Australian GEOGRAPHIC
OUTBACK QUEENSLAND

BIRDS

By Danielle Lancaster

Woodslane Press Pty Ltd
10 Apollo Street
Warriewood, NSW 2102
Email: info@woodslane.com.au
Tel: 02 8445 2300 Website: www.woodslane.com.au

First published in Australia in 2019 by Woodslane Press in association with Australian Geographic
© 2019 Woodslane Press, photographs © Australian Geographic and others
(see acknowledgements on page 62)

A catalogue record for this book is available from the National Library of Australia

Printed in China by KS Printing
Cover image: Sunrise near Winton by Tourism and Events Queensland/Phil Warren
Back cover: canbalci
Book design by: Christine Schiedel and Cory Spence

CONTENTS

OUTBACK QUEENSLAND

■ Right : The Central Bearded Dragon appears more dangerous than it looks. Its flat body shape allows it to hug surfaces when it is lying down to absorb heat. The elongated spinous scales around the rear of the lower jaw and sides of the body look very spiky but are actually quite rubbery and only intended to make the lizard appear unappealing to predators. When walking, it usually seems slow, though when a higher gait is required this beautiful lizard moves with considerable speed. Unfortunately, it has become a sought-after commodity on the black-market for reptile collectors, and this may threaten the species.

■ Above : Sunrise on Cooper Creek at the Dig Tree, the only creek in Australia formed by the joining of two rivers: the Thomson and Barcoo. It was named in 1845 by explorer Charles Sturt during a dry time hence being named a creek. As one of the most famous rivers in Australia, its waters flow and feed into the Lake Eyre Basin.

Queensland's outback was once part of a Great Inland Sea, surrounded by tropical rainforests and harbouring an array of prehistoric creatures roaming in and out of the water. Today the view is vastly different. Within this ancient landscape, rocky outcrops and expansive deserts are dominated by sand and harbour rare plants and animals - many endangered and some found nowhere else on Earth. The region, the largest in Queensland, may at first seem deserted, yet it incorporates a wide range of diverse environments. It boasts one of Australia's oldest dinosaur discoveries, including one of Queensland's eleven World Natural Heritage areas at Riversleigh Fossil Fields, along with a remarkable people, incredible vistas and accounts of incredible deeds. Massive cattle stations are the caretakers of one of Australia's largest organic beef industries and along with isolated towns form an essential part of pioneering history. There are many Australian stories from this area: the famous verse Waltzing Matilda was penned and first performed in Queensland's outback, the Australian Labour Party and QANTAS were formed in Outback Queensland, and Burke and Wills' historic expedition tragically ended along the banks of the Cooper Creek. There are many other stories that continue into the present. Outback Queensland may no longer have the bounties of the sea at its doorstep; however, it does have a diverse array of offerings. As you travel you will be rewarded with a sense of adventure, beautiful scenery stretching from horizon to horizon and new-found friends. You may well find yourself, like many others, coming back time and time again.

OUTBACK QUEENSLAND

Boodjamulla

Four Ways

76

Camooweal

A2

83

83

N

0   100km   200km

63

Townsville

72

A6

A1

Lake
Moondarra

Mount Isa

Cloncurry   Julia Creek   A6   Richmond

Porcupine Gorge

Hughenden   A6

Dalrymple Lake

Riversleigh

McKinlay

A2

62

19

18

Lake Buchanan

77

11

83

Lillyvale Hills

62

Winton

62

QUEENSLAND

Lake Galilee

70

Boulia

83

DIAMANTINA
NATIONAL PARK

Longreach   A2   Barcaldine

19

41

A4

79

Bedourie

Stonehenge

Blackall

A2

Lake
Machattie

12

79

Tambo

Bilpa
Morea
Claypan

83

Windorah

WELLFORD
NATIONAL
PARK

14

Augathella   A2

Betoota

14

CHESTERTON
NATIONAL
PARK

Birdsville

14

Lake
Yamma Yamma

Charleville   A71

A2

Big Red

Eromanga   Quilpie

14

Murweh

SOUTH AUSTRALIA

Innamincka

Dig Tree

LAKE BINDEGOLLY
NATIONAL PARK

A71

Thargomindah

Yowah
Opal Fields

Cunnamulla

49

Bulloo Downs

Cameron Corner

Left: The world's third (following Paris and London) and Australia's first hydro-electric power plant for street lighting was installed in the little outback town of Thargomindah, using water from the Great Artesian Basin.

Below: Road trains – trucks pulling up to three stock crates - are not uncommon on the remote highways. When you see them approaching, give yourself plenty of time to pull off the road and allow them right of away. You will be rewarded with a big wave.

GEOLOGY

O Once upon a time, much of Queensland's outback was part of the Great Inland Sea. Dating over 100 million years ago, much of the continent of Australia was covered by both this gigantic sea and large forested plains, all teeming with wildlife and plant life. The distinctive Channel Country, seen nowhere else in the world, slowly formed. Along the channels, water sluggishly trickles down from rain that has fallen a long way to the north, gently nourishing the lands, feeding the wildlife and stock.

Today the region sits upon the Great Artesian Basin (GAB), the largest and deepest artesian basin in the world, stretching over 1.7 million square kilometres and a last remnant of the Great Inland Sea. The water of the GAB is held within a layer laid down by continental erosion during the Triassic, Jurassic, and early Cretaceous periods. The majority of this sedimentary rock layer is sandstone, siltstone and claystone, perfect for creating fossils and making Outback Queensland one of the most significant places for dinosaur discoveries in the world.

Mesas, not seen anywhere else other than in South America, rise above the landscape around Winton and Middleton. These sites would have been prime real estate positions way back in the day with immaculate sea views. However, time has moved on. Massive stations, friendly towns, outback pubs and dusty golf courses have replaced the sea views. Yabbie and camel races have replaced dinosaur stampedes and below the ground, minerals, oil, gas and gems are carefully harvested. Isolated gorges remain, harbouring prehistoric rain forest pockets and waterfalls.

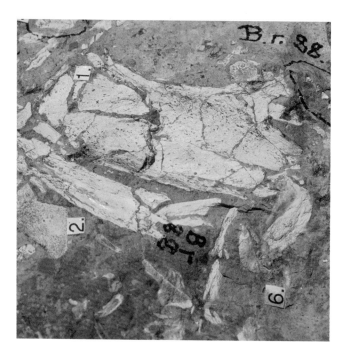

Left: In the Channel Country water traveling down the connecting rivers gently nourishes surrounding soils and revives plants, providing lush fodder for native flora, fauna and stock. The end point is Lake Eyre Basin, Australia's largest lake and the lowest natural point in Australia (approximately 15 metres below sea level).

Opposite page, top: Riversleigh is one of Australia's most famous fossil sites with remains of ancient mammal, birds and reptiles from the Oligocene and Miocene ages continually being discovered.

Opposite page, below: Australian Boulder opals are the second most valuable type of opal (following black opal) and are found only in Queensland's outback. It is an opaque gemstone due to its ironstone content. Created between 50-65 million years ago, it is the modern October birthstone and the accepted gem for 13th wedding anniversaries. Major opal fields include areas around Quilpie, Winton and Yowah.

CLIMATE

Outback Queensland spans both sides of the Tropic of Capricorn. To the north, the area experiences more of a typical monsoonal cycle, with two distinct seasons, the Dry and the Wet, and with a higher humidity than further south. Below this line (23.43679° south) rain is less frequent. Average temperatures in Queensland's outback vary an incredible amount from excessively hot in summer on both sides to below freezing in winter, once you are south of the Tropic.

The land is nourished not only by rain but also water flowing from the north through the phenomenal Channel Country into the south-west of the region. Some of this water will reach Lake Eyre, Australia's largest, covering a massive 9,500 square kilometres. The Channel Country's unique set of creeks and rivers, that look more like a spider web from the air, gently fill and flood the land. The El Niño Southern Oscillation has been associated with seasonal abnormalities in many areas of the world, and outback Queensland is no different. The region can experience long dry droughts, wet periods with floods along with remarkable dust storms that turn the sky to red. Before travelling, it is recommended checking conditions first in any season.

■ Right: A summer storm passes over an outback station, delivering a small amount of rain and cooling temperatures after a long hot day.

SUMMER
■ (December - February)
Summer is the hottest time of the year. Temperatures average 35°C and often reach above 40°C. It's the low season with tourist numbers at their minimum. Many attractions are closed during summer with the long, hot days occasionally broken by a summer storm, which are usually short, isolated and spectacular.

AUTUMN
■ (March - May)
Temperatures start to decrease though can remain warm, with both day and night averaging between 21.5°C and 29°C. In Autumn, traveller numbers slowly increase, as visitors start to make the trip west, and if there has been good rain or waters flowing through the channel country, the wildflowers are often in full bloom. By Easter, most tourist attractions are open.

WINTER
■ (June – August),
Winter, the coldest time in the outback, can see temperatures go below 0°C and frosts forming icicles on the ground overnight. The sun soon melts these as clear blue skies generally follow with warm daytime temperatures meaning you will be pulling off any early morning layers by lunchtime. It's the best time of the year for viewing the stars with less impact from clouds. It is also peak tourist season.

SPRING
■ (September to November)
Temperatures start to slowly build and range on average from 20.5°C to 29°C. Spring marks the end of the tourist season and the birth of new animals. Calves flank their mothers in awe of their new surroundings and recently born joeys peak curiously from their mothers' pouches. Storms are infrequent, often isolated and usually pass quickly.

Above: Children from stations and towns delight in coming together at an event.

Right: Lester McCain at the Middleton Hotel is an excellent example of why you should allow extra time to stop at some of the more isolated places.

Opposite page, bottom left: Dick Loveday pulls up to check the stock he is taking east from Birdsville.

Opposite page, bottom right: The Royal Flying Doctor Service (RFDS) has been supporting the people of the outback for over 90 years. Reverend John Flynn witnessed the daily struggle of pioneers living in remote areas and had a vision to provide a 'mantle of safety' for the people of the bush. Today it continues providing medical treatment for all that live and travel within Outback Queensland.

Outback Queensland's people are often described as 'salt of the earth'. In 1860 the Burke and Wills expedition set off from Melbourne, led by Robert O'Hara Burke and William John Wills along with 8 others, 25 camels, 22 horses and a few wagons. The aim was for the first crossing of Australia from south to north, around 3,250 kilometres. It was ill-fated, with Burke and Wills both dying of starvation in July 1861. John King, the one lone survivor, embraced the indigenous Yantruwanta people, who looked after him until he was found a few months later. Since that day, the indigenous and white settlers of outback Queensland have worked together.

Graziers with herds of cattle and sheep were drawn to the region by reports of grass plains to the height of a horse's flank and flowing rivers. While good seasons do occur, so do the bad, and the people that have stayed and nurtured the land are proof of the stamina required to endure this harsh yet rewarding region. Take the time to stop and chat with a local – you will be dutifully rewarded. As the most isolated area in Queensland, many children from stations do their education via Distance Education, the largest classroom in the world.

The region boasts being the birthplace of QANTAS, the Australian Labour Party and the Royal Flying Doctor Service (RFDS) while the little town of Thargomindah is famous for being the third location after London and Paris to install hydro-electricity. It may be remote, but the people are insightful and use their resources wisely. Events draw the locals together, many travelling hundreds of kilometres to enjoy each other's company. The locals rub shoulders and welcome new visitors like long-time friends.

ECONOMY

Queensland's outback covers around one million square kilometres and has the smallest per capita population of any region in the state. It is home to just over 56,000 people with the population predicted to reach 60,000 by 2036. It encompasses 22 local government areas with the major regional centres being Mount Isa, Charleville, Longreach and Barcaldine. The large grass plains enticed settlers with herds of cattle and sheep and agricultural production contributes close to two billion dollars annually to the economy. It remains the biggest employer in the region with 16.5% of the workforce, followed closely by mining with 15.6%. Mount Isa Mines boasts the largest zinc resource base and the biggest underground network of mines in the world, providing work for more than 3,200 employees and contractors. From the little copper connections in your mobile phone to the zinc used to galvanise industrial steel, much flows from this outback city. Roma in the south, considered one of the gateways to the outback, was the first place in Australia where natural gas was discovered. Tourism remains a major growth industry and the lifeblood for many of the small towns.

Left: A cattle muster at Mt Leonard Station. Outback Queensland produces premium organic beef.

Above: On a tour of the Hard Time Mine, visitors get to descend underground with miners to experience life deep below the surface.

CULTURE

Well before Europeans arrived in Australia, geological understanding of the country by Indigenous Australians was acute. It is estimated the first Australians came here around 50,000 years ago, following routes carved by water and food. To many, it may seem a harsh environment, yet the first settlers on this land found it hospitable and a fulfilling setting providing for their daily needs. They learned to read the weather, the patterns of animals and plants and established elaborate trade arrangements for stone implements across long distances from specific quarry sites such as Mount Isa. It is estimated there are more than 25 indigenous language groups within Outback Queensland. Stories handed down from generation to generation reiterate the Dreamtime and form an essential part of the intricate culture that revolves around 'country', a term that means more than just land. It is life before, now and after. It is everything and celebrates all the intricate ways of how life is lived. Culture, heritage and the natural environment are inseparable. Indigenous culture is displayed in many a city and town as Australia's original proud ancestors cherish long and lasting customs and traditions and its custodians openly welcome you into the heart of Queensland's outback.

Left: The Betoota Serpent is on the traditional lands of the Mithaka People. This artwork represents a series of pathways that connect the river systems in the Channel Country of the Diamantina Shire, and was created using gravel and gibbers found throughout the region.

Opposite page, bottom left: Indigenous Australians were immersed into the outback well before white man arrived. They since have all worked together, forming intricate relationships.

Opposite page, bottom right: The story of the dreaming, culture and the meaning of Country is handed down from generation to generation. Jimmie Crombie shares stories with his nephew Jodi Barr on Australia's largest sand dune in the Simpson Desert, Big Red (original name Nappanerica).

Bottom left: Ancient rock art throughout Outback Queensland portrays the life of the original custodians.

Bottom right: Artworks are created from fibres and natural dyes collected from the lands.

WILDLIFE

While it may seem desolate, Queensland's outback provides a home for an array of wildlife that has evolved to withstand a harsh landscape and challenging climate. Wildlife outnumbers the human population. Travel any road, and you are sure to see many kangaroos and emus, both featured on the Australian coat of arms. Mammals, birds, reptiles and insects all naturally thrive in Outback Queensland, although many have become endangered, such as the Julia Creek Dunnart, a denizen of the Mitchell Grass plains, and in the south, the Greater Bilby. Inland lakes and watercourses form retreats and breeding sanctuaries; many birds are attracted to the waterways and lakes within national parks and on private properties. Currawinya Lakes is a listed Ramsar site preserving wetlands and the animals and plants around them. The region is also the natural habitat of the Inland Taipan, considered the most venomous land snake in the world. One drop of venom, it is said, can kill one million mice. However, it is shy, mostly nocturnal and reclusive, and will only attack to defend itself. A large number of outback animals are nocturnal, so it is best to avoid driving between dusk and dawn. Many roads lead through private property, hence it's not only wildlife but also stock you need to be aware of. Unfortunately, the animals are not aware of road safety and are often drawn to the sides of the road for fresh grass or feeding off road kill.

Opposite page top: The Yellow-footed Rock Wallaby is listed as vulnerable: a small population hangs on in Outback Queensland. Through the 1880s to about 1920 it was hunted in large numbers for its pelt. A striking feature is its tail which is very long and yellow and has rings all the way down it. At the Charleville National Park headquarters, you can see these cute wallabies through their successful breeding program.

Left: Often described as the most beautiful of all cockatoos, the Major Mitchell Cockatoo has a soft-textured white and salmon-pink plumage and large, bright red and yellow crest. It is named in honour of Major Sir Thomas Mitchell, who wrote: "Few birds more enliven the monotonous hues of the Australian forest than this beautiful species whose pink-coloured wings and flowing crest might have embellished the air of a more voluptuous region."

Left: Not a native to Australia, the camel was initially introduced to transport supplies over long distances. Weighing 600–1,000 kilogrammes, they can cover up to 70 kilometres every day. They are used today for the consumption of invasive plants, in annual races that form major events around the outback, and some meat production.

Opposite page, bottom right: Commonly known as the sand goanna, this large monitor lizard is also called the Gould's Monitor, and sometimes you will hear it referred to as the racehorse goanna due to its rapid pace. It is a relentless forager and diurnal, meaning most of its activities take place during the day.

PLANTLIFE

The plants that have set down their roots in Queensland's outback are regarded as some of the most resilient in Australia. Tolerant to droughts and floods, differing species come into flower through all the seasons. The region boasts nearly 5,000 different plant species and an average of 20 new plant species are discovered each year. Blooming cycles are intricately tied to weather patterns and flowers attract an assortment of insects and animals. Rainforest pockets shelter remnants of prehistoric flora around gorges and seasonal waterfalls. Plants shoot when the conditions are suitable, and some seeds may lie dormant for years until the appropriate climatic conditions occur. The further west you travel, trees become shorter, and all pants grow lower to the ground. There are exceptions: Mulga trees, seen in the south-west, provide shelter and food for stock and the western Myall is one of the higher trees growing up to 12 metres and found predominantly in the south. With a widespread canopy, the Myall is an ideal shade tree, and its silvery, needle-like leaves are typical of many trees in the outback. They protect the plants during long dry periods by preventing excessive evaporation. Herbage growing prostate to the ground offers native animals, cattle and sheep, a nutrient-rich food source.

■ Right: The beautiful yellow flowers of the Yapunyah tree are prized by apiarists as they produce nectar in winter when few other plants are in flower. An important food source for native birds particularly the Pied Honeyeater, the wood is suitable for fuel, fencing and construction and the leaves can be used as fodder.

■ Right: Spinifex is commonly found on sand and marginally rocky country. The genus Triodia is a large hummock-forming bunchgrass endemic to Australia. The leaves are very spikey and if they break off into the skin are known to cause infections.

PLANTLIFE

Opposite page, left: Known as either Waddy or Waddi, this tree is only found in three locations in Australia - two in Outback Queensland near Boulia and Birdsville. This very slow growing species - some trees have been dated at 500 years or older - has long spike-like leaves reducing evaporation. The flowers are a pale yellow colour and generally appear in autumn and spring following heavy rain. The wood is incredibly tough and almost impossible to cut. It was used by Indigenous people to produce clubs known as a waddy – hence the name.

Top left: Commonly known as Mulla Mulla or Foxtails, Ptilotus microcephalus is indigenous to Australia. While a relatively rare species, it can be seen flowering from colours of almost pure white to purple.

Top right: Water lilies bloom in various colours from white to deep purple across eastern lagoons.

Left: The Acetosa vesicaria, known as Wild Hops, is not a native flower. This introduced species was accidentally spread by the Afghan cameleers in the mid-1800s. They used the plant to pad out the saddlebags on their camels. Seeds transported soon thrived in the outback.

Following page: Wildflowers in bloom across the sand dunes of the Simpson Desert.

FLINDERS & RICHMOND

This is prime dinosaur country. Both shires are situated on the Overlander's Way and share the Flinders River, Queensland's longest, named in 1841 after Captain Matthew Flinders, which empties into the Gulf of Carpentaria. Today, each region supports proud pastoral communities and tourism-based industries.

On the east is Flinders Shire covering an area of 41,538 square kilometres, more than the size of Tasmania. The principal main administrative centre is Hughenden with the smaller communities of Prairie, Torrens Creek and Stamford forming intricate hubs within the shire. This is the traditional home of the Yirendali Aboriginal people. The area once sat on the shoreline of the great inland sea and is world-renown for over 3,000 terrestrial and marine dinosaur fossil finds. The most famous is 'Hughie', a Muttaburrasaurus. He was the first entire dinosaur skeleton found in Australia.

To the west is the Richmond Shire, located almost halfway between tropical Townsville and Australia's largest outback city, Mount Isa. Traversing 26,602 square kilometres, it was once positioned right under the great inland sea which existed around 100 million years ago and has become world-renowned for its marine fossil finds.

Left: Porcupine Gorge National Park, 60 kilometres north of Hughenden, features towering sandstone cliffs surrounded by flat savanna plains. It's often referred to as Australia's mini Grand Canyon.

Opposite page below: Kronosaurus Korner, in Richmond, is considered a premier marine fossil museum. It features 'Penny' the Richmond plesiosaur (Australia's best vertebrate fossil), 'Krono' (Kronosaurus queenslandicus) – a 10 metre, giant marine reptile and 'Wanda' – Australia's largest fossilised fish, along with 'Mia' (Minmi paravertebral) – considered to be Australia's best-preserved dinosaur skeleton and 'Marlin's Beastie' – a gigantic plant-eating sauropod dinosaur.

Below left: Moon rocks, sometimes referred to as moonstones or dinosaur eggs (though they are neither), are a geological concretion. Although concretions are not fossils themselves, they can sometimes contain fossils and range in size from golf balls to boulders weighing several tonnes.

■ Above: Burke and Wills passed through the region on their epic expedition from Melbourne to the Gulf in 1861. Burke's water bottle is now a major feature at the Cloncurry Museum. There's a dedicated memorial 43 kilometres west of town on the bank of the Corella River.

As you travel west, McKinlay Shire, covering 41,000 square kilometres, incorporates the towns of Julia Creek, McKinlay, Kynuna and the small locality of Nelia. Its total population stands at around 1,000 people. Julia Creek was named after the niece of Donald McIntyre, the first white settler in the area, and its major industries are beef, wool and mining, plus it remains a significant centre for cattle sales and transport. Julia Creek is situated 650 kilometres west of Townsville and 250 kilometres east of Mount Isa on the Flinders Highway, also known as The Overlander's Way. This is the main travelling route from tropical Townsville on the coast, to Tennant Creek in the Northern Territory. With road upgrades to Normanton, Julia Creek has also become known as the "Gateway to the Gulf". Cloncurry Shire lies to the west of McKinlay and only 120 kilometres east of Mount Isa. It boasts a population of around 3,200 with the locals referring to it as 'The Curry'. Founded by Ernest Henry in 1867 with the discovery of copper, Cloncurry's core industries include grazing, transport services, copper and gold mining. Voted Queensland's Friendliest Town in 2013, few places can claim to be as influential in shaping Australia. It is the birthplace of the Royal Flying Doctor Service and made aviation history when QANTAS' first passenger flew from Longreach to Cloncurry in 1922. You can still visit the original hanger. Nearby is the deserted town of the Mary Kathleen Uranium Mine which is now a tourist attraction. The Cloncurry Unearthed Visitor Information Centre should be your first stop with a wealth of information on the area.

Top left: The Mitchell grass plains surrounding the township of Julia Creek are home to the rare and endangered Julia Creek Dunnart (*Sminthopsis douglasi*). This extremely shy, nocturnal but adorable small carnivorous marsupial was rediscovered in 1992 after it was thought to be extinct.

Below left: The popular Dirt n Dust Festival held in Julia Creek annually draws triathletes from across the globe to compete in one of the most difficult and harshest triathlon environments. There are many other events from bull riding to horse races and even the highly unusual bog snorkelling.

MOUNT ISA

Mount Isa is the largest city in outback Australia, with locals simply referring to it as 'The Isa'. Covering a massive 40,977 square kilometres, it claims to be the largest city in area in the world with the main street extending 189 kilometres, finishing in Camooweal to the west. Mount Isa Mines (MIM) is one of the most productive single mines in world history, producing lead, silver, copper and zinc. It employs a large volume of workers in varying fields with copper remaining the main product. It is Australia's deepest and one of the largest underground mines in the world with over 1,000 kilometres of tunnels. The land around the city is home to the Kalkadoon Indigenous peoples. With the ochre-red Selwyn Ranges and the contrasting Leichhardt River, this rugged terrain has become a haven for four-wheel drivers and visitors who want to explore a region much as the first pioneers did many years ago. Twin jewels in Mount Isa's crown are the spectacular Lawn Hill Gorge in Boodjamulla National Park and its neighbour, the world heritage listed Riversleigh Fossil Fields. The region is honeycombed with rare sinkholes and caves, dating back to the Cambrian Period (about 500 million years ago), attracting those experienced in serious caving

■ Above: Located on Hillary Street, the City Lookout offers a 360° panorama across 'The Isa'.

Above: Camooweal, the last Queensland town before the Northern Territory border, on the Barkly Highway, is called the home of drovers as it was once the centre for enormous cattle drives travelling south.

The Mount Isa Mines Rodeo is held every August. It's the world's third largest rodeo and the largest in the Southern Hemisphere, attracting competitors and spectators from the young to the old. In 2018 the Rodeo Hall of Fame opened in Mount Isa, adding another layer to the city's year-round attractions, though there is nothing quite like watching the excitement of a rodeo live.

WINTON

Above: "Once a jolly swagman camped by a billabong..." Winton is where the epic Australian verse, Waltzing Matilda was written. The poem has gone on to become a song, and many an Aussie refers to it as their second national anthem. At the Waltzing Matilda Centre in Winton, you will learn more about this famous verse and the outback region.

Opposite page, top: The township of Middleton, on the western fringe of the Winton Shire, has a population of 2. Take the time to pull over and say hello at the pub when passing by.

Opposite page, bottom: Cawnpore Lookout and its view of the magnifically multi-coloured Lillyvale Hills.

Winton, first settled in 1875, was initially called Pelican Waterhole. It is a vibrant outback town surrounded by extensive grass plains broken by gloriously coloured gorges, ridges and mesas (or, as the locals call them, 'jump-ups').

This is the home of Waltzing Matilda. AB 'Banjo' Patterson is reported to have been inspired to pen the verse by a shearer's suicide in 1894 at the nearby Combo Waterhole while staying at Dagworth Station. He first publicly orated the poem in the North Gregory Hotel on April 6th 1895.

Boulder opals are found nearby at places such as Opalton, Queensland's oldest opal field. Shops in town sell this valuable gemstone at much lower prices than their city cousins. Dinosaur findings have thrown Winton onto the global map. At Lark Quarry are the 93 million-year-old footprints of a dinosaur stampede while the Australian Age of Dinosaurs Museum contains the largest collection of Australian dinosaur fossils in the world. The Museum is split between three facilities, the Fossil Preparation Laboratory, Collection Room and Dinosaur Canyon. Winton played an important role in the forming of QANTAS when on November 16th, 1920 the initial registration of the company was undertaken in this small outback town. The town hosts much eccentricity, like Arno's Wall and the Musical Fence. Willy Marr was the last Chinese gardener in Winton and maybe the whole outback, and his residence is beautifully maintained by the community. The Middleton Hotel, between Winton and Boulia, was built during the Cobb & Co. era. The hotel is said to be one of the most isolated pubs in Queensland, if not Australia and the original hitching rail remains in front of the hotel. Bladensburg National Park, 17 kilometres south-west of Winton includes remarkable outback flora and fauna along with a varied landscape from grassland plains, river flats, sandstone ranges to mesas.

The mysterious and unexplained Min Min Lights that have been witnessed around Boulia were first documented from 1918, though local indigenous mythology indicates the phenomenon was around well before white man came to the area. The Boulia Shire encompasses 62,000 square kilometres, with a population of around 440. Covered predominately with Mitchell and Flinders grass plains, its name is said to be derived from a waterhole on the Burke River named Bulla Bulla by the local Pitta Pitta indigenous people. Venture behind Boulia's historic Stonehouse into a fascinating locally found fossil display where you'll see the carefully preserved skeletons of marine reptiles such as the longnecked Plesiosaur, the Kronosaurus and the Icthyosaur. Fishing for Yellowbelly and Redclaw at Parapituri Waterhole, the Police Barracks Waterhole and in the Burke River have become drawcards for visitors along with the annual camel races.

Left: The Boulia Camel Races is the richest professional camel meet in Queensland and the longest camel race in Australia, running a 1500-metre cup final. These 'Ships of the Desert' race on the third weekend of July each year.

Above: Windmills have generated a means to bring water above ground, and this grand old windmill in the main street of Boulia delivered water for the town right up until the 1970s.

Right: Venture behind the Stone House and discover what life was like when this region was part of the Great Inland Sea.

Far right: Ghostly orbs of light have been fascinating people for centuries around Boulia. At the Min Min Encounter, a theatrical experience in Boulia, you'll learn more about these intriguing lights.

BARCALDINE & LONGREACH

n Barcaldine, known as the Garden City of the West, every street is named after a tree. The town name originates from the Oban region in Scotland, however, the town is most famous as the birthplace of the Australian Labour Party. Barcy, as it's referred to by the locals, boasts five pubs along the main street alone (not bad for a town of 1,300 souls) – a reminder of the great shearing days – so you won't be lost for a place to quench your thirst. Driving around town, you'll see along with the many beautiful gardens, heritage-listed buildings like the Masonic Lodge, built in 1901. It is an unusual design: while it was built from tin and timber, it's been painted to look like it's made from stone. Longreach Shire is situated 700 kilometres from the coast, west of Rockhampton, and covers an area of 40,638 square kilometres – a bit over half the size of Tasmania. The shire includes the townships of Longreach, Ilfracombe, Isisford and Yaraka with an entire population of approximately 3,600. Situated on the Tropic of Capricorn, the primary industries are cattle, sheep and tourism. Longreach is the central hub and was named after the "long reach" of the Thomson River which sits close to town.

Longreach, one of the founding centres for QANTAS, the third oldest airline in the world, boasts the QANTAS Founders Outback Museum where you can walk out on the wing of a decommissioned plane or merely take in the history of this airline that started its flying days in humble outback Queensland. The town has become a stepping stone for further outback experiences as it's linked by air, rail and sealed roads. A spectacular sunset along the mighty Thompson River, which eventually feeds into the Lake Eyre basin, is a great way to start or end an outback adventure.

Above left: The historic Wellshot Hotel is located in the small town of Ilfracombe, less than 30 kilometres east of Longreach. The pub found its permanent home in Ilfracombe in 1890 after being relocated several times by bullock and cart as the railway line into the west was established. The hotel could be called a museum as it displays a large amount of local memorabilia - and it also serves hearty meals.

Above right: Above right: The Tree of Knowledge sits outside Barcaldine railway station and is best known as the birthplace of the Australian Labour Party and the location of the first Australian shearer's strike. It was once a flourishing ghost gum that was sadly poisoned in 2006. Today it stands as a marvellous piece of public art in the form of a sculpture comprising 4,913 different timbers.

Above: The Australian Stockman's Hall of Fame in Longreach was officially opened in 1988 by Queen Elizabeth II. It pays tribute to the many people who worked together in forming todays Queensland outback culture including indigenous and pioneering men and women.

Following page: Another magnificent outback sunset.

BLACKALL & TAMBO

Settled on the banks of the Barcoo River, this region is renowned for 'growing on the sheep's back'. The Barcoo River joins the Thomson River to form Cooper Creek, east of Windorah, with the water ultimately flowing into Lake Eyre Basin.

Wool has been an important industry since the first white settlers came to the area. In Tambo, along with the beautiful heritage buildings and streets lined with native bottle trees is Tambo Teddies. This local business was initially set up to assist regional sheep farmers hit hard by climate, and economic changes and has today grown into a major tourist attraction.

In Blackall, the historic Blackall Woolscour is the last remaining scour in Australia and forms a museum on how the industry developed. Blackall is the home of the legendary Jackie Howe, a national icon who sheared 321 sheep on the nearby Alice Downs in 7 hours and 40 minutes, using manual blade shears. Jackie went on to be the publican of the Barcoo Hotel in Blackall, and his record remained unbroken for 58 years. The Jackie Howe navy blue singlet, designed for him by his mother for easier shearing, soon became famous and today is still sold in large numbers in both the outback and city.

Above: The Blackall Sculpture Trail has been created by many acclaimed artists working alongside local residents inspired by the stories of the region. Different art works form this fascinating trail, such as this huge steel ball on the outskirts of town.

Left: Locals work together forming innovative businesses such as Tambo Teddies have created a source of income as a bulwark against tough times.

■ Left: The Blackall Woolscour operated from 1908 through until 1978. Woolscouring means wool washing, and this is the only steam-driven scour incorporating a shearing shed left in Australia.

THE BARCOO

Above: The sand hills, 12 kilometres to the west of Windorah, will probably be the deepest natural red you will ever see. Animal tracks and plants abound in this exceptional environment that harbours precious flora and fauna.

Right: Right: When he was eight-years old, Tarpot earned his unique nickname because of his jet-black hair. Today that is all he is known by, though there maybe a few more silver flecks scattered across his scalp. He spent his whole life as a drover, and now resides in Windorah, in what was once Windorah's one-room courthouse.

Far right: The Barcoo boasts being the only place in outback Queensland where two prominent inland rivers, the Thomson and Barcoo, meet to form a 'creek': Cooper Creek, located 35 kilometres south of Windorah.

I n the heart of the Channel Country, the Barcoo region encompasses 61,974 square kilometres, close to the size of Tasmania. Within the shire are the three towns of Windorah, Jundah and Stonehenge, all easily accessed via sealed roads. Windorah is an Aboriginal word meaning 'Big Fish'. An original slab hut, circa 1906, built on the banks of the Whitula Creek has been relocated to the Visitor Information Centre and forms the centrepiece of the Whitula Gate Museum. The JC pub ruins are 80 kilometres west of Windorah, and while not much remains, the cemetery is a moving reminder of the early pioneers. A massive solar power farm supplies most of Windorah's energy requirements. A local highlight is Cooper Creek, as Windorah sits near a deep permanent waterhole lined with massive Red River Gums: perfect for camping, birdwatching and fishing. Jundah, the administration centre for the Shire is another revered location for avid birdwatchers and anglers. Unique 'Welcome Signs' into town replicate a historic shopfront still standing in the main street. Along with the historical site of Magee's Shanty, from Banjo Patterson's Bush Christening (located around 100 kilometres to the southeast), is also a native well 32 kilometres north of Jundah on the Stonehenge road, a cherished water supply for the indigenous people. Wellford National Park, covering 124,000 hectares, protects a spinifex ecology, red sand hills, mulga lands and resplendent waterholes rich with wildlife. Stonehenge is only 151 kilometres from Longreach. To sign the visitor's book is simple, you stop and make your name in stone directly beside the main road!

DIAMANTINA SHIRE

Covering a massive 95,000 square kilometres – one and a half times the size of Tasmania - Diamantina Shire lies in far southwestern Queensland. It is bordered to one side by the Simpson Desert, the fourth-largest desert in Australia. Sprinkled with only three intriguing farflung towns, Birdsville, Betoota and Bedourie, it has a rich history and is home to only 11 stations and 300 residents. The country may seem harsh as it is a land of extremes, yet it supports an amazing variety of wildlife and plants, and is regarded as having the best organic cattle fattening land in Australia. Forming part of the Channel Country, a large amount of the region is sometimes flooded through a web-like affect from rain received much further north. This soaks the countryside and forms ideal conditions for plants to grow and animals to prosper. Birdsville lays claim to one of the most famous pubs in Australia and the second most famous horse racing meet in Australia - the Birdsville Races. The ruins of the Royal Hotel, bore and billabong (with a large bird population), and the bakery - with its pies from curried camel to kangaroo and claret - are a few of the highlights. Standing over 40 metres in height, Big Red is Australia's highest sand dune and is situated approximately 35 kilometres west of Birdsville on the edge of Munga-Thirri National Park, formally the Simpson Desert NP. It's the first of 1,140 parallel dunes that run across the Simpson Desert..

Bedourie, meaning 'dust storm' is perched on a sand dune supporting around 120 people and is the administrative centre for the shire. It's the birthplace of the Bedourie Camp Oven, created under a tree in the 1920s and the perfect oven for camp fire cooking. Within town, the historic Mud Hut is believed to be one of the first buildings constructed in town. The cemetery and the sculpture in Herbert Street are also worthy of viewing.

In contrast Betoota stands on a vast gibber plain, 170 kilometres east of Birdsville, and receives an annual rainfall of just 300 millimetres. It may look almost like a ghost town, but it erupts twice a year with the Horse and Motorbike Gymkhana on the first weekend of the Queensland Easter school holidays, and the races in August which commence the Simpson Desert Racing Carnival. Other attractions in the shire include Carcoory Ruins, Vaughan Johnson Lookout, Deons Lookout, Diamantina National Park and the wetlands of Cuttuburra Crossing.

Above left: The Birdsville Races sees the town's population increase from 200 to over 7,000.

Left: No one visits Birdsville without calling into the iconic hotel.

Following page: The Simpson Desert surrounds the tiny of town of Birdsville. It has become a legendary destination enticing both those that like an off-road adventure and nature enthusiasts.

WELCOME TO
QUEENSLAND'S OUTBACK
LARGER THAN LIFE

Warrego Highway

Charleville 🛈 222

MURWEH

Above: The Warrego Highway starts at the Sunshine State's capital, Brisbane, and finishes 766 kilometres west in Charleville.

Top right: Cooladdi is the smallest town in this expansive shire. Once a bustling railway town it is now home to only a few. The remaining railway siding is one of the most photographed buildings in the region. The Foxtrap Roadhouse is an all-in-one store, pub, post office and motel.

Middle right: Its big sky country and at the Cosmos Centre by day and night you'll discover amazing facts about the night sky that humans have always looked up in awe at since man first walked on Earth.

Bottom right: The heritage-listed Hotel Corones in Charleville is a fine example of a grand old outback pub. The doors first opened in 1929, and the hotel was built by Harry "Poppa" Corones, who from being a poor 17-year-old migrant became the first Greek hotel licensee in Australia.

Murweh Shire, and its towns, Charleville, Morven, Augathella and Cooladdi, is situated on the Great Artesian Basin and covers 43,905 square kilometres. The shire is home to just under 5,000 people, with sheep and cattle the primary industries.

Charleville is the central hub and sits on the banks of the Warrego River at the junction of the Mitchell and Warrego Highways. Explorer, Edmund Kennedy was the first white man into the area in 1847, and the town's first surveyor came from Charleville, Ireland, hence the town's name. The original inhabitants were the Bidjara Aboriginal people, and it is thought the name Murweh means waterhole.

Morven, to the east of Charleville, is only 10 kilometres from Tregole National Park. A short walking track explains the plants and wildlife including the rare Ooline trees dating from the Pleistocene Era and protected within the park. Augathella lays claim to be Meat Ant Country, and in the Meat Ant Park, there's a giant sculpture over a million times the size of an actual ant. Murals and sculptors around the town showcase the diverse artistic community. There is much to see and do including Chesterton Range National Park, Morven Conservation Park, and the Charleville Bilby Experience. In 1942, American Soldiers arrived in Charleville and commandeered Charleville airport to set up a secret base. Today you can learn more about this interesting part of Charleville's history on a Top Secret WWII Tour. There's plenty of accommodation but a favourite for many is camping under the stars that stretch forever and forever.

■ Travel the lesser travelled road in outback Queensland and you'll be astonished at the characters and sights you'll discover.

QUILPIE

Quilpie Shire is steeped in history and natural attractions. Covering 67,633 square kilometres, the shire incorporates the towns of Eromanga, Toompine, Cheepie and Adavale. The region is home to the largest dinosaur found in Australia, beautiful national parks and boulder opal fields to name a few of its attractions. Adavale, once the centre of the Adavale Shire, and Cheepie, which was a Cobb & Co change station from 1914, and now almost a ghost town, allows those that make it out here to experience something very different. Eromanga is the furthest town from the ocean in Australia and produces 1.5 million barrels of oil per year. Significant dinosaurs have been unearthed and the area is being heralded by scientists as the most exciting and prolific dinosaur site in Australia, with new dinosaurs being named including George, Cooper (the largest dinosaur in Australia), Zac (one of the most complete dinosaurs unearthed in Australia) and Sid (named after Sir Sydney Kidman). The Eromanga Natural History Museum has all the information on these miraculous finds.

Left: The views over the countryside, such as from Baldy Top Lookout on the outskirts of Quilpie, are simply divine.

Below: Below: Toompine is one of the smallest towns in the shire and could possibly boast the smallest public bar in Australia. A short distance from the hotel is a historic cemetery – unfortunately the sign writer at the time wasn't great at spelling! With graves from young to old, it is a legacy from the times gone by.

xplorer William Landsborough recognised the potential opportunity within the Paroo region when he passed through the area in 1862. With fertile plains and river flats, he identified ideal grazing lands for sheep and cattle. Today, these industries continue to have a pivotal role in the economy of the district. It's another huge area, encompassing 47, 727 kilometres and with a population of around 1,860. The main commercial centre is Cunnamulla with the townships of Eulo, Wyandra and Yowah surrounding it. Industries are varied within the shire and include sheep for wool and meat, cattle, goats, macropod harvesting, opals and honey. Sheltered on, the banks of the Warrego River, Cunnamulla (meaning 'long stretch of water') is located at the crossroads of the Mitchell Highway and the Adventure Way. The shire is a bird watching and fishing hot spot. At the Cunnamulla Visitor Centre, the Artesian Time Tunnel takes you on a journey back 100 million years ago when not only dinosaurs roamed the earth but precious underground gems like opals were being formed.

Far left: The Yowah opal fields, 132 kilometres west of Cunnamulla, is the southernmost opal mining centre in western Queensland and has become famous for the occurrence of precious opal in siliceous ironstone nodules, generally referred to as Yowah Nuts.

Left: The SpongeBob mailbox welcomes you to Wandilla Station, south of Eulo, where every May Music in the Mulga attracts hundreds of people.

Below: The Eulo Queen became a legend of the outback, and the pub in Eulo is named in honour of the thrice-married pub owner, storekeeper and opal trader, Isabel Gray. According to folklore, she was attempting to eject an unruly drinker, and roared: "I'm the Eulo Queen – now get out!"

BULLOO SHIRE

overing an area of 73,807 square kilometres, Bulloo Shire's hub is the town of Thargomindah, approximately 1,000 kilometres west of Brisbane. Thargo, as the locals call it, was the third town in the world after London and Paris to produce hydroelectricity. The shire supports the towns of Thargomindah (population 255), Hungerford (population 12), Noccundra (population 2) and Oontoo (population 0). It is home to Lake Bindegolly and Currawinya National Parks, each nurturing rare outback flora and fauna. Lake Bindegolly National Park, 40 kilometres east of Thargomindah, covers 14,000 hectares and encompasses a series of lakes: Bindegolly, Toomaroo and Hutchinson. The lakes join to form a body of water after heavy rainfall and at times thousands of waterbirds flock to this inland oasis to feed and breed. With a range of environments from samphire flats, claypans, sand dunes, hard and soft red mulga country, gidgee woodlands, and Eremophila shrublands, the park was established to protect the Acacia ammophila tree, threatened with extinction. Currawinya, near Hungerford, is the traditional home of the Budjiti People and recent acquisitions bring the national park's total area to around 344,000 hectares, making it one of Queensland's largest. In the west, on the banks of Cooper Creek, is the Burke and Wills Dig Tree on Nappa Merrie station. The Dig Tree at Coolibah is believed to be between 200-250 years old and has become a national icon, although unfortunately the blazes are now almost unrecognisable. Long roads lead to Cameron Corner, on the border with South Australia and New South Wales, and the Corner Post – the official meeting of these three states. The Dog Fence, the longest man-made structure in the world, runs along the southern border of the shire protecting southern flocks of sheep from 'wild dogs' – don't forget to shut the gate. In Hungerford and Noccundra, heritage listed pubs open their doors to welcome you into their sliver of the outback. With hitching rails still in place from the days of visitors by horse, they now embrace the modern-day traveller who takes the time to stop.

Above: Lake Numalla, in Currawinya National Park, is one of the many sites in the park protecting thousands of years of Aboriginal culture, pastoral history and threatened wildlife. It is Ramsar listed due to its importance as a wetland.

Left: The Face Tree, located roughly 30 metres downstream of the Dig Tree, shows a carving of Robert O'Hara Burke, who died while making the first south-north crossing of Australia. Carved by John Dick in 1898, it is still clearly visible. Burke's grave is a little further downstream near Innamincka.

■ Norley Woolshed, on private property, is one of the woolsheds still standing from the days of large sheep grazing and shearing crews in the shire. There is another in Currawinya National Park which is open to the public.

ACKNOWLEDGEMENTS

The author would like to thank all the talented photographers who submitted images for selection. She would like to particularly thank Andrew Swaffer and Christine Schiedel at Woodslane, Shelley Winkel from Tourism Events and Queensland, Tracy Wattz, Lorraine Kath, Lea Macken, Rod Fensham and many others for their valuable fact checking with plants, animals and the magical environs of outback Queensland, an area we all dearly love, plus the crew at Australian Geographic.

ABOUT THE AUTHOR

Danielle Lancaster is the author of the award-winning '4WD treks Close to Brisbane' along with 'Out around the Bulloo' and 'Tropical Queensland and the Great Barrier Reef', another Australian Geographic title. Born and bred in Queensland, there is not much of her home state she has not seen. Working as a travel writer and photographer for domestic and international publications, Danielle is the past president of the Australian Society of Travel Writers and a founding member for the formation of the Global Travel Writers and Media Association. She won a Walkley award for her slide show 'Healing Cambodia's Wounds'. Danielle, along with writing, teaches, runs photography tours and does public speaking engagements through her company Bluedog. www.blue-dog.com.au

ABOUT THE PUBLISHERS

The Australian Geographic journal is a geographical magazine founded in 1986. It mainly covers stories about Australia - its geography, culture, wildlife and people - and six editions are published every year. Australian Geographic also publish a number of books every year on similar subjects for both children and adults. A portion of the profits goes to the Australian Geographic Society which supports scientific research as well as environmental conservation, community projects and Australian adventurers. www.australiangeographic.com.au.

Woodslane Press is a book publishing company based in Sydney, Australia. It is the publisher of Australia's best-selling walking guides and under its co-owned Boiling Billy imprint also publishes camping, bush exploration and 4WD guides. For more than a decade committed to publishing books that empower Australians to better explore and understand their own country, Woodslane Press is proud to be working with Australian Geographic to produce this new series of souvenir books. www.woodslane.com.au.

Also available:

 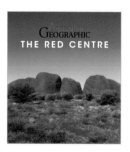 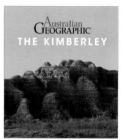

PICTURE CREDITS

All images are protected by copyright and have been reproduced with permission.

Front cover: Tourism and Events Queensland
pi: Danielle Lancaster
pii: Danielle Lancaster
p1: Danielle Lancaster
p2: Danielle Lancaster (top); Lea Macken (bottom)
p5: Danielle Lancaster (top & bottom)
p6-7: Lorraine Kath/Outback Photography
p6: Tourism and Events Queensland/Peter Lik (top); Danielle Lancaster (bottom)
p8-9: Danielle Lancaster
p10: Lorraine Kath/Outback Photography (top); Danielle Lancaster (bottom)
p11: Danielle Lancaster (top, bottom left & right)
p12-13: Lorraine Kath/Outback Photography
p13: Danielle Lancaster
p14-15: Lorraine Kath/Outback Photography (top
p14: Danielle Lancaster (all images)
p15: Tourism and Events Queensland/ Peter Lik (bottom left); Danielle Lancaster (bottom right)
p16: Danielle Lancaster
p17: Danielle Lancaster (all images)
p18: Danielle Lancaster (top); Lea Macken (bottom)
p19: Lea Macken (top); Danielle Lancaster (bottom)
p20: Danielle Lancaster

p21: Danielle Lancaster
p22-23: Danielle Lancaster (all images)
p24-25: Tourism and Events Queensland
p26-27: Tourism and Events Queensland/ Ezra Patchett
p26-27: Tourism and Events Queensland/Murray Waite & Associates
p 27: Danielle Lancaster (bottom left)
p28: Danielle Lancaster
p29: Danielle Lancaster (top); Tourism and Events Queensland/Simon Grimmett (bottom)
p30: Danielle Lancaster
p31: Danielle Lancaster
p32-33: Tourism and Events Queensland/ Stephen Mowbray
p34: Tourism and Events Queensland/Caroline & Craig Makepeace
p35: Danielle Lancaster (top and bottom)
p36: Tourism and Events Queensland/ Steve Holland
p37: Danielle Lancaster (all images)
p38: Danielle Lancaster (left); Paul Ewart (right)
p39: Tourism and Events Queensland/Peter Lik
p40-41: Tourism and Events Queensland
p42-43: Danielle Lancaster

p42: Tourism and Events Queensland/ Caroline & Craig Makepeace (bottom)
p43: Tourism and Events Queensland
p44: Danielle Lancaster
p45: Danielle Lancaster (left)/Tourism and Events Queensland (right)
p46: Danielle Lancaster
p47: Tourism and Events Queensland/Reichlyn Aguilar (top); Danielle Lancaster (bottom)
p48-49: Danielle Lancaster
p50: Danielle Lancaster
p51: Danielle Lancaster (top); Tourism and Events Queensland/Chris McLennan (middle & bottom)
p52-53: Danielle Lancaster
p54: Tourism and Events Queensland/ Ezra Patchett
p55: Danielle Lancaster
p56: Tourism and Events Queensland/ Ezra Patchett
p57: Danielle Lancaster (top); Tourism and Events Queensland/Peter Lik
p58: Danielle Lancaster
p59: Danielle Lancaster
p60-61: Danielle Lancaster
Back cover: Danielle Lancaster